THE PADDLER'S PLANNER

THE PADDLER'S PLANNER

by

Patricia J. Bell

Eden Prairie, Minnesota

To Friend Spouse Don — ever my favorite canoe partner

Copyright ©1989 Patricia J. Bell

Cover Design by Bruce Harrington

International Standard Book Number 0-9618227-3-2

All rights reserved. No part of this book may be used or reproduced in any manner whatsoever without written permission except in the case of brief quotations embodied in critical articles and reviews. For information address Cat's-paw Press, 9561 Woodridge Circle, Eden Prairie, Minnesota 55347.

First printing, 1989

0 9 8 7 6 5 4 3 2

Printed in the United States of America

THE PADDLER'S PLANNER

TABLE OF CONTENTS

HOW TO USE THIS BOOK 1

MASTER CHECK LIST 5

TRIP LOG 18

FOOD SUGGESTIONS 169

STAPLES 173

OUR EQUIPMENT LIST 177

REMINDERS 181

ADDRESSES 185

HOW TO USE THIS BOOK

Perle Mesta, the Hostess With the Mostest, was famed for her parties. Napoleon was noted for his brilliant strategy. The key to success for both was planning. Canoe camping trips, like any other trips, go better if the home work has been carefully done, and that is what this book is about.

Part of the pleasure of wilderness camping derives from the fact that life is pretty well uncluttered. You are concerned with food, warmth, and shelter. Your planning aims at securing those elements, and so you insure a certain amount of enjoyment because you have planned well.

Whether you are a beginner or a veteran canoe camper, keeping a record of each trip provides a basis of experience that will make planning later trips easier. What's more, it will enhance the recollection of those trips.

This book aims to do two things: to help you organize your trip and to provide a record of the trip itself. *The Paddler's Planner* can help you focus your thinking **before** you go. Use the MASTER CHECK LISTS to help you select gear for a pleasant trip and to organize the usual camping, clothing, cooking gear, health and safety kits in a systematic manner. Each list has a space for three trips, with a place for the date to identify which trip you are listing.

The Paddler's Planner is designed primarily for the wilderness paddler. Wilderness canoe camping calls for rather strict attention to keeping the load as light as possible. Think "efficient" and "light" when selecting gear and food for such a trip. If you are thinking of carrying other items not on the list, think about what can do double duty. Many wilderness areas have restrictions against bottles and cans, and that will be a definite factor in planning food as well. Other areas of the country may have characteristics that call for some things different. Add these items to the MASTER CHECK LIST to make this book your own.

Two, use the TRIP LOG for recording the details of a trip. Faithfully recording each trip gives you specific information (and you don't have to strain your memory!) that will help you make later trip planning easier and more efficient. You can record not only when and where the trip took place, but how long it was, who went, and remarks about the weather conditions. Further, use it as a journal to record sights, thoughts and experiences. You'll remember more if you made a note of it.

NOTES FOR NEXT TIME lets you to "debrief" on the trip — what went well, what you tried that was different and how it worked, things you'd do differently or take if you were going on that trip again, how difficult the trip was, et cetera.

In the TRIP LOG you can record details about meals — what you took, how much, and what members of the party thought about it. Better still, you can use *The Paddler's Planner* to lay out menus on a daily basis before you go. You'll find FOOD SUGGESTIONS of foods you can find in the supermarket and that work well for trips in addition to, or in place of, trail foods. Beginners may welcome the suggestions. Veteran campers may also find them useful simply as a means from getting stuck in a rut. STAPLES is a general list of basic items useful in preparing a meal yet don't need to be listed in the daily menus. Write in specific quantities for trips of specific length and party size for useful reference on later trips.

You probably have read other books on canoe camping, maybe even made many trips. You may know you don't need to buy everything at once. But when you do buy equipment, OUR EQUIPMENT LIST is a convenient place to note when you bought it and what its cost was.

The REMINDERS section is a place to note the date of a completed trip, repairs or replacements in gear that are needed, or equipment items that you should or would like to get.

ADDRESSES is the place to jot down special addresses, such as where to write for permits or reservations, names of outfitters, or anybody else you may need to contact for planning that next trip.

Finally, NOTES are there for those times you need more space for comments.

Use and enjoy!

MASTER CHECK LIST

To Be Used For Every Trip

(date)   (date)   (date)

_____	_____	_____	Permits/reservations
_____	_____	_____	Maps
_____	_____	_____	Licenses
_____	_____	_____	Other
_____	_____	_____	Canoe
_____	_____	_____	Paddles
_____	_____	_____	Personal flotation devices
_____	_____	_____	Canoe bailer, where required
_____	_____	_____	Tent
_____	_____	_____	Small whiskbroom
_____	_____	_____	Ground Cloth
_____	_____	_____	Tarp or large (about 9 x 12') plastic sheet with grommets
_____	_____	_____	20' rope for ridgepole
_____	_____	_____	100' 1/4 in. nylon cord for corners
_____	_____	_____	Sleeping bag
_____	_____	_____	Mattress
_____	_____	_____	Packs
_____	_____	_____	10' rope (1/4 in.), misc.
_____	_____	_____	Bear rope, 2 35'-50' pieces
_____	_____	_____	Clothes pins (12)
_____	_____	_____	Saw (folding)
_____	_____	_____	Flashlight
_____	_____	_____	Compass
_____	_____	_____	Plastic bags
_____	_____	_____	Notebook and pen

Optional

(date)   (date)   (date)

_____ _____ _____ Space Blanket™
_____ _____ _____ Pillow
_____ _____ _____ Camp shovel or backpacker's trowel
_____ _____ _____ Hatchet with sheath
_____ _____ _____ Food cooler
_____ _____ _____ Map envelope
_____ _____ _____ Small back pack
_____ _____ _____ Binoculars
_____ _____ _____ Fishing gear
_____ _____ _____ Lantern (candle or gas)
_____ _____ _____ String hammock
_____ _____ _____ Sun Shower™
_____ _____ _____ Books or other "playthings"
_____ _____ _____ Photographic equipment

COOKING EQUIPMENT

_____ _____ _____ Cook kit (nested kettles)
_____ _____ _____ Eating utensils (forks, spoons)
_____ _____ _____ Plates or bowls
_____ _____ _____ Cups
_____ _____ _____ Pancake turner or spatula
_____ _____ _____ Canteen or water bottle
_____ _____ _____ Collapsible water jug
_____ _____ _____ Pot scrubber
_____ _____ _____ Dish towels
_____ _____ _____ Matches (waterproof case), butane
                          lighter
_____ _____ _____ Pot holders or oven mitts
_____ _____ _____ Portable stove
_____ _____ _____ Fuel container for stove
_____ _____ _____ Filter funnel, if stove requires
_____ _____ _____ Aluminum foil
_____ _____ _____ Long-handled spoon

REPAIRS KIT

(date)   (date)   (date)

_____ _____ _____ Duct tape
_____ _____ _____ Emery board or nail file
_____ _____ _____ Nail clippers
_____ _____ _____ Needle and thread
_____ _____ _____ Safety pins (or in Health and Safety Kit)
_____ _____ _____ Small scissors (not nail or cuticle)
_____ _____ _____ Tweezers

HEALTH AND SAFETY KIT

_____ _____ _____ Aspirin or aspirin substitute
_____ _____ _____ Antihistamine
_____ _____ _____ Antacid
_____ _____ _____ Water purification means
_____ _____ _____ Antiseptic or antibiotic cream
_____ _____ _____ Cortisone ointment (0.5% hydrocortisone)
_____ _____ _____ Topical analgesic
_____ _____ _____ Eye drops
_____ _____ _____ Personal prescribed medications
_____ _____ _____ Band-aids™, assorted sizes
_____ _____ _____ Telfa™ pads, assorted sizes
_____ _____ _____ Gauze and tape
_____ _____ _____ Safety pins, assorted sizes
_____ _____ _____ Splint, rigid or inflatable (for joint injuries)
_____ _____ _____ Triangle bandage
_____ _____ _____ Pre-moistened towelettes (optional)
_____ _____ _____ Whistle
_____ _____ _____ Small mirror
_____ _____ _____ Personal identification tags

CLOTHING

(date)	(date)	(date)	
_____	_____	_____	Sturdy pants; shorts optional
_____	_____	_____	Tee shirts or tank tops
_____	_____	_____	Long-sleeved shirt
_____	_____	_____	Nylon wind-breaker or shell jacket
_____	_____	_____	Woolen or chamois unlined jacket/ shirt
_____	_____	_____	Underwear (number of sets)
_____	_____	_____	Sleepwear
_____	_____	_____	Thick socks (number of pairs)
_____	_____	_____	Shoes: trail shoes and camp shoes
_____	_____	_____	Rain gear
_____	_____	_____	Hat
_____	_____	_____	Sunglasses
_____	_____	_____	Gloves (optional, according to season)
_____	_____	_____	Toothbrush and dentifrice
_____	_____	_____	Soap
_____	_____	_____	Towels
_____	_____	_____	Toilet paper
_____	_____	_____	Sunscreen
_____	_____	_____	Insect repellent
_____	_____	_____	Lip protection
_____	_____	_____	Knife, sharpening stone
_____	_____	_____	
_____	_____	_____	
_____	_____	_____	

MASTER CHECK LIST

To Be Used For Every Trip

(date)   (date)   (date)

_____ _____ _____ Permits/reservations

_____ _____ _____ Maps

_____ _____ _____ Licenses

_____ _____ _____ Other

_____ _____ _____ Canoe

_____ _____ _____ Paddles

_____ _____ _____ Personal flotation devices

_____ _____ _____ Canoe bailer, where required

_____ _____ _____ Tent

_____ _____ _____ Small whiskbroom

_____ _____ _____ Ground Cloth

_____ _____ _____ Tarp or large (about 9 x 12') plastic
sheet with grommets

_____ _____ _____ 20' rope for ridgepole

_____ _____ _____ 100' 1/4 in. nylon cord for corners

_____ _____ _____ Sleeping bag

_____ _____ _____ Mattress

_____ _____ _____ Packs

_____ _____ _____ 10' rope (1/4 in.), misc.

_____ _____ _____ Bear rope, 2 35'-50' pieces

_____ _____ _____ Clothes pins (12)

_____ _____ _____ Saw (folding)

_____ _____ _____ Flashlight

_____ _____ _____ Compass

_____ _____ _____ Plastic bags

_____ _____ _____ Notebook and pen

Optional

(date)   (date)   (date)

_____ _____ _____ Space Blanket™
_____ _____ _____ Pillow
_____ _____ _____ Camp shovel or backpacker's trowel
_____ _____ _____ Hatchet with sheath
_____ _____ _____ Food cooler
_____ _____ _____ Map envelope
_____ _____ _____ Small back pack
_____ _____ _____ Binoculars
_____ _____ _____ Fishing gear
_____ _____ _____ Lantern (candle or gas)
_____ _____ _____ String hammock
_____ _____ _____ Sun Shower™
_____ _____ _____ Books or other "playthings"
_____ _____ _____ Photographic equipment

COOKING EQUIPMENT

_____ _____ _____ Cook kit (nested kettles)
_____ _____ _____ Eating utensils (forks, spoons)
_____ _____ _____ Plates or bowls
_____ _____ _____ Cups
_____ _____ _____ Pancake turner or spatula
_____ _____ _____ Canteen or water bottle
_____ _____ _____ Collapsible water jug
_____ _____ _____ Pot scrubber
_____ _____ _____ Dish towels
_____ _____ _____ Matches (waterproof case), butane
                           lighter
_____ _____ _____ Pot holders or oven mitts
_____ _____ _____ Portable stove
_____ _____ _____ Fuel container for stove
_____ _____ _____ Filter funnel, if stove requires
_____ _____ _____ Aluminum foil
_____ _____ _____ Long-handled spoon

REPAIRS KIT

(date)   (date)   (date)

_____	_____	_____	Duct tape
_____	_____	_____	Emery board or nail file
_____	_____	_____	Nail clippers
_____	_____	_____	Needle and thread
_____	_____	_____	Safety pins (or in Health and Safety Kit)
_____	_____	_____	Small scissors (not nail or cuticle)
_____	_____	_____	Tweezers

HEALTH AND SAFETY KIT

_____	_____	_____	Aspirin or aspirin substitute
_____	_____	_____	Antihistamine
_____	_____	_____	Antacid
_____	_____	_____	Water purification means
_____	_____	_____	Antiseptic or antibiotic cream
_____	_____	_____	Cortisone ointment (0.5% hydrocortisone)
_____	_____	_____	Topical analgesic
_____	_____	_____	Eye drops
_____	_____	_____	Personal prescribed medications
_____	_____	_____	Band-aids™, assorted sizes
_____	_____	_____	Telfa™ pads, assorted sizes
_____	_____	_____	Gauze and tape
_____	_____	_____	Safety pins, assorted sizes
_____	_____	_____	Splint, rigid or inflatable (for joint injuries)
_____	_____	_____	Triangle bandage
_____	_____	_____	Pre-moistened towelettes (optional)
_____	_____	_____	Whistle
_____	_____	_____	Small mirror
_____	_____	_____	Personal identification tags

CLOTHING

(date)	(date)	(date)	
_____	_____	_____	Sturdy pants; shorts optional
_____	_____	_____	Tee shirts or tank tops
_____	_____	_____	Long-sleeved shirt
_____	_____	_____	Nylon wind-breaker or shell jacket
_____	_____	_____	Woolen or chamois unlined jacket/ shirt
_____	_____	_____	Underwear (number of sets)
_____	_____	_____	Sleepwear
_____	_____	_____	Thick socks (number of pairs)
_____	_____	_____	Shoes: trail shoes and camp shoes
_____	_____	_____	Rain gear
_____	_____	_____	Hat
_____	_____	_____	Sunglasses
_____	_____	_____	Gloves (optional, according to season)
_____	_____	_____	Toothbrush and dentifrice
_____	_____	_____	Soap
_____	_____	_____	Towels
_____	_____	_____	Toilet paper
_____	_____	_____	Sunscreen
_____	_____	_____	Insect repellent
_____	_____	_____	Lip protection
_____	_____	_____	Knife, sharpening stone
_____	_____	_____	_____
_____	_____	_____	_____
_____	_____	_____	_____

MASTER CHECK LIST

To Be Used For Every Trip

(date)   (date)   (date)

_____	_____	_____	Permits/reservations
_____	_____	_____	Maps
_____	_____	_____	Licenses
_____	_____	_____	Other
_____	_____	_____	Canoe
_____	_____	_____	Paddles
_____	_____	_____	Personal flotation devices
_____	_____	_____	Canoe bailer, where required
_____	_____	_____	Tent
_____	_____	_____	Small whiskbroom
_____	_____	_____	Ground Cloth
_____	_____	_____	Tarp or large (about 9 x 12') plastic sheet with grommets
_____	_____	_____	20' rope for ridgepole
_____	_____	_____	100' 1/4 in. nylon cord for corners
_____	_____	_____	Sleeping bag
_____	_____	_____	Mattress
_____	_____	_____	Packs
_____	_____	_____	10' rope (1/4 in.), misc.
_____	_____	_____	Bear rope, 2 35'-50' pieces
_____	_____	_____	Clothes pins (12)
_____	_____	_____	Saw (folding)
_____	_____	_____	Flashlight
_____	_____	_____	Compass
_____	_____	_____	Plastic bags
_____	_____	_____	Notebook and pen

Optional

(date)   (date)   (date)

- Space Blanket™
- Pillow
- Camp shovel or backpacker's trowel
- Hatchet with sheath
- Food cooler
- Map envelope
- Small back pack
- Binoculars
- Fishing gear
- Lantern (candle or gas)
- String hammock
- Sun Shower™
- Books or other "playthings"
- Photographic equipment

COOKING EQUIPMENT

- Cook kit (nested kettles)
- Eating utensils (forks, spoons)
- Plates or bowls
- Cups
- Pancake turner or spatula
- Canteen or water bottle
- Collapsible water jug
- Pot scrubber
- Dish towels
- Matches (waterproof case), butane lighter
- Pot holders or oven mitts
- Portable stove
- Fuel container for stove
- Filter funnel, if stove requires
- Aluminum foil
- Long-handled spoon

REPAIRS KIT

(date)   (date)   (date)

(date)	(date)	(date)	
_____	_____	_____	Duct tape
_____	_____	_____	Emery board or nail file
_____	_____	_____	Nail clippers
_____	_____	_____	Needle and thread
_____	_____	_____	Safety pins (or in Health and Safety Kit)
_____	_____	_____	Small scissors (not nail or cuticle)
_____	_____	_____	Tweezers

HEALTH AND SAFETY KIT

_____	_____	_____	Aspirin or aspirin substitute
_____	_____	_____	Antihistamine
_____	_____	_____	Antacid
_____	_____	_____	Water purification means
_____	_____	_____	Antiseptic or antibiotic cream
_____	_____	_____	Cortisone ointment (0.5% hydrocortisone)
_____	_____	_____	Topical analgesic
_____	_____	_____	Eye drops
_____	_____	_____	Personal prescribed medications
_____	_____	_____	Band-aids™, assorted sizes
_____	_____	_____	Telfa™ pads, assorted sizes
_____	_____	_____	Gauze and tape
_____	_____	_____	Safety pins, assorted sizes
_____	_____	_____	Splint, rigid or inflatable (for joint injuries)
_____	_____	_____	Triangle bandage
_____	_____	_____	Pre-moistened towelettes (optional)
_____	_____	_____	Whistle
_____	_____	_____	Small mirror
_____	_____	_____	Personal identification tags

CLOTHING

(date)   (date)   (date)

_____	_____	_____	Sturdy pants; shorts optional
_____	_____	_____	Tee shirts or tank tops
_____	_____	_____	Long-sleeved shirt
_____	_____	_____	Nylon wind-breaker or shell jacket
_____	_____	_____	Woolen or chamois unlined jacket/ shirt
_____	_____	_____	Underwear (number of sets)
_____	_____	_____	Sleepwear
_____	_____	_____	Thick socks (number of pairs)
_____	_____	_____	Shoes: trail shoes and camp shoes
_____	_____	_____	Rain gear
_____	_____	_____	Hat
_____	_____	_____	Sunglasses
_____	_____	_____	Gloves (optional, according to season)
_____	_____	_____	Toothbrush and dentifrice
_____	_____	_____	Soap
_____	_____	_____	Towels
_____	_____	_____	Toilet paper
_____	_____	_____	Sunscreen
_____	_____	_____	Insect repellent
_____	_____	_____	Lip protection
_____	_____	_____	Knife, sharpening stone
_____	_____	_____	
_____	_____	_____	
_____	_____	_____	

NOTES

TRIP LOG

Dates of trip: Day:

Who went?

Map(s) needed:

License, permit or reservation needed:

Day's starting point:

Ending point:

Area or length of trip:

Weather conditions:

Comments:

FOOD

BREAKFAST

LUNCH

DINNER

SNACKS AND EXTRAS

Notes for next time:

TRIP LOG

Dates of trip: Day:

Who went?

Map(s) needed:

License, permit or reservation needed:

Day's starting point:

Ending point:

Area or length of trip:

Weather conditions:

Comments:

FOOD

BREAKFAST

LUNCH

DINNER

SNACKS AND EXTRAS

Notes for next time:

TRIP LOG

Dates of trip: Day:

Who went?

Map(s) needed:

License, permit or reservation needed:

Day's starting point:

Ending point:

Area or length of trip:

Weather conditions:

Comments:

FOOD

BREAKFAST

LUNCH

DINNER

SNACKS AND EXTRAS

Notes for next time:

TRIP LOG

Dates of trip: Day:

Who went?

Map(s) needed:

License, permit or reservation needed:

Day's starting point:

Ending point:

Area or length of trip:

Weather conditions:

Comments:

FOOD

BREAKFAST

LUNCH

DINNER

SNACKS AND EXTRAS

Notes for next time:

TRIP LOG

Dates of trip: Day:

Who went?

Map(s) needed:

License, permit or reservation needed:

Day's starting point:

Ending point:

Area or length of trip:

Weather conditions:

Comments:

FOOD

BREAKFAST

LUNCH

DINNER

SNACKS AND EXTRAS

Notes for next time:

TRIP LOG

Dates of trip: Day:

Who went?

Map(s) needed:

License, permit or reservation needed:

Day's starting point:

Ending point:

Area or length of trip:

Weather conditions:

Comments:

FOOD

BREAKFAST

LUNCH

DINNER

SNACKS AND EXTRAS

Notes for next time:

TRIP LOG

Dates of trip: Day:

Who went?

Map(s) needed:

License, permit or reservation needed:

Day's starting point:

Ending point:

Area or length of trip:

Weather conditions:

Comments:

FOOD

BREAKFAST

LUNCH

DINNER

SNACKS AND EXTRAS

Notes for next time:

TRIP LOG

Dates of trip: Day:

Who went?

Map(s) needed:

License, permit or reservation needed:

Day's starting point:

Ending point:

Area or length of trip:

Weather conditions:

Comments:

FOOD

BREAKFAST

LUNCH

DINNER

SNACKS AND EXTRAS

Notes for next time:

TRIP LOG

Dates of trip: Day:

Who went?

Map(s) needed:

License, permit or reservation needed:

Day's starting point:

Ending point:

Area or length of trip:

Weather conditions:

Comments:

FOOD

BREAKFAST

LUNCH

DINNER

SNACKS AND EXTRAS

Notes for next time:

TRIP LOG

Dates of trip: Day:

Who went?

Map(s) needed:

License, permit or reservation needed:

Day's starting point:

Ending point:

Area or length of trip:

Weather conditions:

Comments:

FOOD

BREAKFAST

LUNCH

DINNER

SNACKS AND EXTRAS

Notes for next time:

TRIP LOG

Dates of trip: Day:

Who went?

Map(s) needed:

License, permit or reservation needed:

Day's starting point:

Ending point:

Area or length of trip:

Weather conditions:

Comments:

FOOD

BREAKFAST

LUNCH

DINNER

SNACKS AND EXTRAS

Notes for next time:

TRIP LOG

Dates of trip: Day:

Who went?

Map(s) needed:

License, permit or reservation needed:

Day's starting point:

Ending point:

Area or length of trip:

Weather conditions:

Comments:

FOOD

BREAKFAST

LUNCH

DINNER

SNACKS AND EXTRAS

Notes for next time:

TRIP LOG

Dates of trip: Day:

Who went?

Map(s) needed:

License, permit or reservation needed:

Day's starting point:

Ending point:

Area or length of trip:

Weather conditions:

Comments:

FOOD

BREAKFAST

LUNCH

DINNER

SNACKS AND EXTRAS

Notes for next time:

TRIP LOG

Dates of trip: Day:

Who went?

Map(s) needed:

License, permit or reservation needed:

Day's starting point:

Ending point:

Area or length of trip:

Weather conditions:

Comments:

FOOD

BREAKFAST

LUNCH

DINNER

SNACKS AND EXTRAS

Notes for next time:

TRIP LOG

Dates of trip: Day:

Who went?

Map(s) needed:

License, permit or reservation needed:

Day's starting point:

Ending point:

Area or length of trip:

Weather conditions:

Comments:

FOOD

BREAKFAST

LUNCH

DINNER

SNACKS AND EXTRAS

Notes for next time:

TRIP LOG

Dates of trip: Day:

   Who went?

   Map(s) needed:

License, permit or reservation needed:

Day's starting point:

Ending point:

Area or length of trip:

Weather conditions:

Comments:

FOOD

BREAKFAST

LUNCH

DINNER

SNACKS AND EXTRAS

Notes for next time:

TRIP LOG

Dates of trip: Day:

Who went?

Map(s) needed:

License, permit or reservation needed:

Day's starting point:

Ending point:

Area or length of trip:

Weather conditions:

Comments:

FOOD

BREAKFAST

LUNCH

DINNER

SNACKS AND EXTRAS

Notes for next time:

TRIP LOG

Dates of trip: Day:

Who went?

Map(s) needed:

License, permit or reservation needed:

Day's starting point:

Ending point:

Area or length of trip:

Weather conditions:

Comments:

FOOD

BREAKFAST

LUNCH

DINNER

SNACKS AND EXTRAS

Notes for next time:

TRIP LOG

Dates of trip: Day:

Who went?

Map(s) needed:

License, permit or reservation needed:

Day's starting point:

Ending point:

Area or length of trip:

Weather conditions:

Comments:

FOOD

BREAKFAST

LUNCH

DINNER

SNACKS AND EXTRAS

Notes for next time:

TRIP LOG

Dates of trip: Day:

Who went?

Map(s) needed:

License, permit or reservation needed:

Day's starting point:

Ending point:

Area or length of trip:

Weather conditions:

Comments:

FOOD

BREAKFAST

LUNCH

DINNER

SNACKS AND EXTRAS

Notes for next time:

TRIP LOG

Dates of trip: Day:

Who went?

Map(s) needed:

License, permit or reservation needed:

Day's starting point:

Ending point:

Area or length of trip:

Weather conditions:

Comments:

FOOD

BREAKFAST

LUNCH

DINNER

SNACKS AND EXTRAS

Notes for next time:

TRIP LOG

Dates of trip: Day:

Who went?

Map(s) needed:

License, permit or reservation needed:

Day's starting point:

Ending point:

Area or length of trip:

Weather conditions:

Comments:

FOOD

BREAKFAST

LUNCH

DINNER

SNACKS AND EXTRAS

Notes for next time:

TRIP LOG

Dates of trip: Day:

Who went?

Map(s) needed:

License, permit or reservation needed:

Day's starting point:

Ending point:

Area or length of trip:

Weather conditions:

Comments:

FOOD

BREAKFAST

LUNCH

DINNER

SNACKS AND EXTRAS

Notes for next time:

TRIP LOG

Dates of trip: Day:

Who went?

Map(s) needed:

License, permit or reservation needed:

Day's starting point:

Ending point:

Area or length of trip:

Weather conditions:

Comments:

FOOD

BREAKFAST

LUNCH

DINNER

SNACKS AND EXTRAS

Notes for next time:

TRIP LOG

Dates of trip: Day:

Who went?

Map(s) needed:

License, permit or reservation needed:

Day's starting point:

Ending point:

Area or length of trip:

Weather conditions:

Comments:

FOOD

BREAKFAST

LUNCH

DINNER

SNACKS AND EXTRAS

Notes for next time:

TRIP LOG

Dates of trip: Day:

Who went?

Map(s) needed:

License, permit or reservation needed:

Day's starting point:

Ending point:

Area or length of trip:

Weather conditions:

Comments:

FOOD

BREAKFAST

LUNCH

DINNER

SNACKS AND EXTRAS

Notes for next time:

TRIP LOG

Dates of trip: Day:

Who went?

Map(s) needed:

License, permit or reservation needed:

Day's starting point:

Ending point:

Area or length of trip:

Weather conditions:

Comments:

FOOD

BREAKFAST

LUNCH

DINNER

SNACKS AND EXTRAS

Notes for next time:

TRIP LOG

Dates of trip: Day:

   Who went?

   Map(s) needed:

License, permit or reservation needed:

Day's starting point:

Ending point:

Area or length of trip:

Weather conditions:

Comments:

FOOD

BREAKFAST

LUNCH

DINNER

SNACKS AND EXTRAS

Notes for next time:

TRIP LOG

Dates of trip: Day:

Who went?

Map(s) needed:

License, permit or reservation needed:

Day's starting point:

Ending point:

Area or length of trip:

Weather conditions:

Comments:

FOOD

BREAKFAST

LUNCH

DINNER

SNACKS AND EXTRAS

Notes for next time:

TRIP LOG

Dates of trip: Day:

Who went?

Map(s) needed:

License, permit or reservation needed:

Day's starting point:

Ending point:

Area or length of trip:

Weather conditions:

Comments:

FOOD

BREAKFAST

LUNCH

DINNER

SNACKS AND EXTRAS

Notes for next time:

TRIP LOG

Dates of trip: Day:

Who went?

Map(s) needed:

License, permit or reservation needed:

Day's starting point:

Ending point:

Area or length of trip:

Weather conditions:

Comments:

FOOD

BREAKFAST

LUNCH

DINNER

SNACKS AND EXTRAS

Notes for next time:

TRIP LOG

Dates of trip: Day:

Who went?

Map(s) needed:

License, permit or reservation needed:

Day's starting point:

Ending point:

Area or length of trip:

Weather conditions:

Comments:

FOOD

BREAKFAST

LUNCH

DINNER

SNACKS AND EXTRAS

Notes for next time:

TRIP LOG

Dates of trip: Day:

Who went?

Map(s) needed:

License, permit or reservation needed:

Day's starting point:

Ending point:

Area or length of trip:

Weather conditions:

Comments:

FOOD

BREAKFAST

LUNCH

DINNER

SNACKS AND EXTRAS

Notes for next time:

TRIP LOG

Dates of trip: Day:

Who went?

Map(s) needed:

License, permit or reservation needed:

Day's starting point:

Ending point:

Area or length of trip:

Weather conditions:

Comments:

FOOD

BREAKFAST

LUNCH

DINNER

SNACKS AND EXTRAS

Notes for next time:

TRIP LOG

Dates of trip: Day:

Who went?

Map(s) needed:

License, permit or reservation needed:

Day's starting point:

Ending point:

Area or length of trip:

Weather conditions:

Comments:

FOOD

BREAKFAST

LUNCH

DINNER

SNACKS AND EXTRAS

Notes for next time:

TRIP LOG

Dates of trip: Day:

  Who went?

  Map(s) needed:

License, permit or reservation needed:

Day's starting point:

Ending point:

Area or length of trip:

Weather conditions:

Comments:

FOOD

BREAKFAST

LUNCH

DINNER

SNACKS AND EXTRAS

Notes for next time:

TRIP LOG

Dates of trip: Day:

Who went?

Map(s) needed:

License, permit or reservation needed:

Day's starting point:

Ending point:

Area or length of trip:

Weather conditions:

Comments:

FOOD

BREAKFAST

LUNCH

DINNER

SNACKS AND EXTRAS

Notes for next time:

TRIP LOG

Dates of trip: Day:

   Who went?

   Map(s) needed:

License, permit or reservation needed:

Day's starting point:

Ending point:

Area or length of trip:

Weather conditions:

Comments:

FOOD

BREAKFAST

LUNCH

DINNER

SNACKS AND EXTRAS

Notes for next time:

TRIP LOG

Dates of trip: Day:

   Who went?

   Map(s) needed:

License, permit or reservation needed:

Day's starting point:

Ending point:

Area or length of trip:

Weather conditions:

Comments:

FOOD

BREAKFAST

LUNCH

DINNER

SNACKS AND EXTRAS

Notes for next time:

TRIP LOG

Dates of trip: Day:

   Who went?

   Map(s) needed:

License, permit or reservation needed:

Day's starting point:

Ending point:

Area or length of trip:

Weather conditions:

Comments:

FOOD

BREAKFAST

LUNCH

DINNER

SNACKS AND EXTRAS

Notes for next time:

TRIP LOG

Dates of trip: Day:

Who went?

Map(s) needed:

License, permit or reservation needed:

Day's starting point:

Ending point:

Area or length of trip:

Weather conditions:

Comments:

FOOD

BREAKFAST

LUNCH

DINNER

SNACKS AND EXTRAS

Notes for next time:

TRIP LOG

Dates of trip: Day:

Who went?

Map(s) needed:

License, permit or reservation needed:

Day's starting point:

Ending point:

Area or length of trip:

Weather conditions:

Comments:

FOOD

BREAKFAST

LUNCH

DINNER

SNACKS AND EXTRAS

Notes for next time:

TRIP LOG

Dates of trip: Day:

Who went?

Map(s) needed:

License, permit or reservation needed:

Day's starting point:

Ending point:

Area or length of trip:

Weather conditions:

Comments:

FOOD

BREAKFAST

LUNCH

DINNER

SNACKS AND EXTRAS

Notes for next time:

TRIP LOG

Dates of trip: Day:

Who went?

Map(s) needed:

License, permit or reservation needed:

Day's starting point:

Ending point:

Area or length of trip:

Weather conditions:

Comments:

FOOD

BREAKFAST

LUNCH

DINNER

SNACKS AND EXTRAS

Notes for next time:

TRIP LOG

Dates of trip: Day:

Who went?

Map(s) needed:

License, permit or reservation needed:

Day's starting point:

Ending point:

Area or length of trip:

Weather conditions:

Comments:

FOOD

BREAKFAST

LUNCH

DINNER

SNACKS AND EXTRAS

Notes for next time:

TRIP LOG

Dates of trip: Day:

Who went?

Map(s) needed:

License, permit or reservation needed:

Day's starting point:

Ending point:

Area or length of trip:

Weather conditions:

Comments:

FOOD

BREAKFAST

LUNCH

DINNER

SNACKS AND EXTRAS

Notes for next time:

TRIP LOG

Dates of trip: Day:

Who went?

Map(s) needed:

License, permit or reservation needed:

Day's starting point:

Ending point:

Area or length of trip:

Weather conditions:

Comments:

FOOD

BREAKFAST

LUNCH

DINNER

SNACKS AND EXTRAS

Notes for next time:

TRIP LOG

Dates of trip: Day:

Who went?

Map(s) needed:

License, permit or reservation needed:

Day's starting point:

Ending point:

Area or length of trip:

Weather conditions:

Comments:

FOOD

BREAKFAST

LUNCH

DINNER

SNACKS AND EXTRAS

Notes for next time:

TRIP LOG

Dates of trip: Day:

Who went?

Map(s) needed:

License, permit or reservation needed:

Day's starting point:

Ending point:

Area or length of trip:

Weather conditions:

Comments:

FOOD

BREAKFAST

LUNCH

DINNER

SNACKS AND EXTRAS

Notes for next time:

TRIP LOG

Dates of trip: Day:

Who went?

Map(s) needed:

License, permit or reservation needed:

Day's starting point:

Ending point:

Area or length of trip:

Weather conditions:

Comments:

FOOD

BREAKFAST

LUNCH

DINNER

SNACKS AND EXTRAS

Notes for next time:

TRIP LOG

Dates of trip: Day:

Who went?

Map(s) needed:

License, permit or reservation needed:

Day's starting point:

Ending point:

Area or length of trip:

Weather conditions:

Comments:

FOOD

BREAKFAST

LUNCH

DINNER

SNACKS AND EXTRAS

Notes for next time:

TRIP LOG

Dates of trip: Day:

Who went?

Map(s) needed:

License, permit or reservation needed:

Day's starting point:

Ending point:

Area or length of trip:

Weather conditions:

Comments:

FOOD

BREAKFAST

LUNCH

DINNER

SNACKS AND EXTRAS

Notes for next time:

TRIP LOG

Dates of trip: Day:

Who went?

Map(s) needed:

License, permit or reservation needed:

Day's starting point:

Ending point:

Area or length of trip:

Weather conditions:

Comments:

FOOD

BREAKFAST

LUNCH

DINNER

SNACKS AND EXTRAS

Notes for next time:

TRIP LOG

Dates of trip: Day:

Who went?

Map(s) needed:

License, permit or reservation needed:

Day's starting point:

Ending point:

Area or length of trip:

Weather conditions:

Comments:

FOOD

BREAKFAST

LUNCH

DINNER

SNACKS AND EXTRAS

Notes for next time:

TRIP LOG

Dates of trip: Day:

Who went?

Map(s) needed:

License, permit or reservation needed:

Day's starting point:

Ending point:

Area or length of trip:

Weather conditions:

Comments:

FOOD

BREAKFAST

LUNCH

DINNER

SNACKS AND EXTRAS

Notes for next time:

TRIP LOG

Dates of trip: Day:

Who went?

Map(s) needed:

License, permit or reservation needed:

Day's starting point:

Ending point:

Area or length of trip:

Weather conditions:

Comments:

FOOD

BREAKFAST

LUNCH

DINNER

SNACKS AND EXTRAS

Notes for next time:

TRIP LOG

Dates of trip: Day:

Who went?

Map(s) needed:

License, permit or reservation needed:

Day's starting point:

Ending point:

Area or length of trip:

Weather conditions:

Comments:

FOOD

BREAKFAST

LUNCH

DINNER

SNACKS AND EXTRAS

Notes for next time:

TRIP LOG

Dates of trip: Day:

Who went?

Map(s) needed:

License, permit or reservation needed:

Day's starting point:

Ending point:

Area or length of trip:

Weather conditions:

Comments:

FOOD

BREAKFAST

LUNCH

DINNER

SNACKS AND EXTRAS

Notes for next time:

TRIP LOG

Dates of trip: Day:

Who went?

Map(s) needed:

License, permit or reservation needed:

Day's starting point:

Ending point:

Area or length of trip:

Weather conditions:

Comments:

FOOD

BREAKFAST

LUNCH

DINNER

SNACKS AND EXTRAS

Notes for next time:

TRIP LOG

Dates of trip: Day:

Who went?

Map(s) needed:

License, permit or reservation needed:

Day's starting point:

Ending point:

Area or length of trip:

Weather conditions:

Comments:

FOOD

BREAKFAST

LUNCH

DINNER

SNACKS AND EXTRAS

Notes for next time:

TRIP LOG

Dates of trip: Day:

Who went?

Map(s) needed:

License, permit or reservation needed:

Day's starting point:

Ending point:

Area or length of trip:

Weather conditions:

Comments:

FOOD

BREAKFAST

LUNCH

DINNER

SNACKS AND EXTRAS

Notes for next time:

TRIP LOG

Dates of trip: Day:

Who went?

Map(s) needed:

License, permit or reservation needed:

Day's starting point:

Ending point:

Area or length of trip:

Weather conditions:

Comments:

FOOD

BREAKFAST

LUNCH

DINNER

SNACKS AND EXTRAS

Notes for next time:

TRIP LOG

Dates of trip: Day:

Who went?

Map(s) needed:

License, permit or reservation needed:

Day's starting point:

Ending point:

Area or length of trip:

Weather conditions:

Comments:

FOOD

BREAKFAST

LUNCH

DINNER

SNACKS AND EXTRAS

Notes for next time:

TRIP LOG

Dates of trip: Day:

Who went?

Map(s) needed:

License, permit or reservation needed:

Day's starting point:

Ending point:

Area or length of trip:

Weather conditions:

Comments:

FOOD

BREAKFAST

LUNCH

DINNER

SNACKS AND EXTRAS

Notes for next time:

TRIP LOG

Dates of trip: Day:

  Who went?

  Map(s) needed:

License, permit or reservation needed:

Day's starting point:

Ending point:

Area or length of trip:

Weather conditions:

Comments:

FOOD

BREAKFAST

LUNCH

DINNER

SNACKS AND EXTRAS

Notes for next time:

TRIP LOG

Dates of trip: Day:

Who went?

Map(s) needed:

License, permit or reservation needed:

Day's starting point:

Ending point:

Area or length of trip:

Weather conditions:

Comments:

FOOD

BREAKFAST

LUNCH

DINNER

SNACKS AND EXTRAS

Notes for next time:

TRIP LOG

Dates of trip: Day:

Who went?

Map(s) needed:

License, permit or reservation needed:

Day's starting point:

Ending point:

Area or length of trip:

Weather conditions:

Comments:

FOOD

BREAKFAST

LUNCH

DINNER

SNACKS AND EXTRAS

Notes for next time:

TRIP LOG

Dates of trip: Day:

   Who went?

   Map(s) needed:

License, permit or reservation needed:

Day's starting point:

Ending point:

Area or length of trip:

Weather conditions:

Comments:

FOOD

BREAKFAST

LUNCH

DINNER

SNACKS AND EXTRAS

Notes for next time:

TRIP LOG

Dates of trip: Day:

   Who went?

   Map(s) needed:

License, permit or reservation needed:

Day's starting point:

Ending point:

Area or length of trip:

Weather conditions:

Comments:

FOOD

BREAKFAST

LUNCH

DINNER

SNACKS AND EXTRAS

Notes for next time:

TRIP LOG

Dates of trip: Day:

Who went?

Map(s) needed:

License, permit or reservation needed:

Day's starting point:

Ending point:

Area or length of trip:

Weather conditions:

Comments:

FOOD

BREAKFAST

LUNCH

DINNER

SNACKS AND EXTRAS

Notes for next time:

TRIP LOG

Dates of trip: Day:

Who went?

Map(s) needed:

License, permit or reservation needed:

Day's starting point:

Ending point:

Area or length of trip:

Weather conditions:

Comments:

FOOD

BREAKFAST

LUNCH

DINNER

SNACKS AND EXTRAS

Notes for next time:

TRIP LOG

Dates of trip: Day:

Who went?

Map(s) needed:

License, permit or reservation needed:

Day's starting point:

Ending point:

Area or length of trip:

Weather conditions:

Comments:

FOOD

BREAKFAST

LUNCH

DINNER

SNACKS AND EXTRAS

Notes for next time:

TRIP LOG

Dates of trip: Day:

Who went?

Map(s) needed:

License, permit or reservation needed:

Day's starting point:

Ending point:

Area or length of trip:

Weather conditions:

Comments:

FOOD

BREAKFAST

LUNCH

DINNER

SNACKS AND EXTRAS

Notes for next time:

TRIP LOG

Dates of trip: Day:

Who went?

Map(s) needed:

License, permit or reservation needed:

Day's starting point:

Ending point:

Area or length of trip:

Weather conditions:

Comments:

FOOD

BREAKFAST

LUNCH

DINNER

SNACKS AND EXTRAS

Notes for next time:

TRIP LOG

Dates of trip: Day:

Who went?

Map(s) needed:

License, permit or reservation needed:

Day's starting point:

Ending point:

Area or length of trip:

Weather conditions:

Comments:

FOOD

BREAKFAST

LUNCH

DINNER

SNACKS AND EXTRAS

Notes for next time:

NOTES

FOOD SUGGESTIONS

Supermarkets are great sources of food supplies for canoe trips if you don't have access to a good camping supply store, or don't want to order supplies. Here are some suggestions that work well on wilderness trips. These are items that pack well, are durable yet tasty, and can manage without refrigeration for at least a day or two.

Breakfast

Bagels
Cinnamon (toast) rusks
English muffins
Rusks, zwieback
Pop-tarts™ or similar breakfast bars
Pumpkin or zucchini bread
Steamed date bread
Pancakes (made from baking mix)
Coffee cake (made from baking mix)
Biscuits or fry bread (made from baking mix)
Cereal, cold — individual packets
Cereal, instant cooked — oatmeal, farina, mixed grains
Granola
Hash-brown potatoes
Dried fruits, cooked — apples, apricots, banana slices, pears, pineapple, golden and black raisins, combinations
Jelly, marmalade, preserves or honey (use for pancakes)
Cocoa (combine cocoa mix and powdered milk)
Coffee (fresh ground or instant)
Tea (tea bags, plain or specialty, or instants; also flavored instants)

169

Lunch

Beef jerky or beef sticks
Dry salami
Summer sausage
String cheese (a type of Mozzarella)
Cheese spreads (tube cheese or small tubs)
Cheese and crackers, snack packs
Peanut butter and crackers, snack packs
Bagels or bagel sticks
Italian bread sticks
Salad crackers of various sorts
Rye crackers
Pilot biscuits
Pita
Whole wheat or stoned wheat crackers
Hard rolls such as French rolls or Kaiser buns
White, whole-wheat or rye bread
Zweiback
Dessert items (see Snacks list)
Fruit drink mix

Dinners

Potato dishes (au gratin, hash-browns, scalloped)
Casserole-type meals
Macaroni and cheese
Pasta and sauce dishes
Raviolini or tortellini (dehydrated)
Falafel
Instant mashed potatoes
Pilaf (packaged rice and vegetable combinations)
Quick-cooking rice, singly or in combination
Ramen noodles
Edam or similar hard cheese
Country ham or Prosciutto
Instant soup
Vegetables — peas, mushrooms, carrots, green beans, black
  Chinese mushrooms, sun-dried corn (requires soaking)
Breads (see Breakfast and Lunch lists)
Corn muffins (use prepared mix)
Apple streusel (dried apple base)
Fruit compote (dried fruits — see Breakfast list)
Instant puddings
Gelatin desserts
Packaged cookies
Fruit bars or packaged brownies
Beverages (see Breakfast, Lunch lists)
Instant flavored coffee drinks
Bouillon cubes

Snacks

Chocolate bars
Dried fruits such as dates, figs, raisins, bananas
Fruit leather
Graham crackers
Granola bars
Halvah
Hard candies
Milk bars
Mixed nuts and seeds (cashews, peanuts, pecans,
   walnuts,pistachios, pumpkin seeds, sunflower seeds, soy nuts)
Stuffed dates
Trail Mix variations
Yogurt bar
Yogurt-covered raisins or peanuts
Vanilla wafers

STAPLES

(Where appropriate, write in quantity taken)

_____ Oil
_____ Salt and pepper
_____ Oleomargarine
_____ Baking mix
_____ Cocoa mix
_____ Fruit-flavored drink powder
_____ Dried milk
_____ Bouillon cubes
_____ Corn meal for dredging fish
_____ Lemon juice
_____ Cinnamon sugar
_____ Marshmallows
_____ Nuts for snacks or for cooking
_____ Raisins for snacks or cooking

Notes:

STAPLES

(Where appropriate, write in quantity taken)

_____	Oil
_____	Salt and pepper
_____	Oleomargarine
_____	Baking mix
_____	Cocoa mix
_____	Fruit-flavored drink powder
_____	Dried milk
_____	Bouillon cubes
_____	Corn meal for dredging fish
_____	Lemon juice
_____	Cinnamon sugar
_____	Marshmallows
_____	Nuts for snacks or for cooking
_____	Raisins for snacks or cooking

Notes:

STAPLES

(Where appropriate, write in quantity taken)

_____	Oil
_____	Salt and pepper
_____	Oleomargarine
_____	Baking mix
_____	Cocoa mix
_____	Fruit-flavored drink powder
_____	Dried milk
_____	Bouillon cubes
_____	Corn meal for dredging fish
_____	Lemon juice
_____	Cinnamon sugar
_____	Marshmallows
_____	Nuts for snacks or for cooking
_____	Raisins for snacks or cooking

Notes:

NOTES

OUR EQUIPMENT LIST

	COST	DATE ACQUIRED
Canoe	_____	_____
Paddles	_____	_____
Personal Flotation Devices,	_____	_____
one per person	_____	_____
one per person	_____	_____
one per person	_____	_____
Tent	_____	_____
Small whiskbroom	_____	_____
Ground cloth	_____	_____
Tarp	_____	_____
Sleeping bag	_____	_____
Mattress	_____	_____
Sleeping bag	_____	_____
Mattress	_____	_____
Sleeping bag	_____	_____
Mattress	_____	_____
Sleeping bag	_____	_____
Mattress	_____	_____
Rope	_____	_____
Pack	_____	_____
Pack	_____	_____
Pack	_____	_____
Dry bag	_____	_____
Dry bag	_____	_____
Dry bag	_____	_____
Shovel or trowel	_____	_____
Saw	_____	_____
Flashlight	_____	_____
Compass	_____	_____
	_____	_____
	_____	_____
	_____	_____

Optional Items

	COST	DATE ACQUIRED
Space Blanket™	_____	_____
Pillow	_____	_____
Hatchet with sheath	_____	_____
Map envelope	_____	_____
Small back pack	_____	_____
Binoculars	_____	_____
Lantern (candle or gas)	_____	_____
String hammock	_____	_____
Collapsible shovel	_____	_____
Sun Shower™	_____	_____
Fishing gear	_____	_____
Food cooler	_____	_____
Photographic equipment	_____	_____
Other items for regular use	_____	_____
	_____	_____
	_____	_____

FOOD PREPARATION GEAR

Cook kit	_____	_____
Eating utensils	_____	_____
Plates or bowls	_____	_____
Cups	_____	_____
Canteen or water bottle	_____	_____
Collapsible water jug	_____	_____
Portable stove	_____	_____
Fuel container for stove	_____	_____
Filter funnel (if needed)	_____	_____

HEALTH AND SAFETY KIT

	COST	DATE ACQUIRED
Water purification means		
Splint		
Whistle		
Personal identification tags		

CLOTHING AND PERSONAL GEAR

	COST	DATE ACQUIRED
Nylon wind-breaker or shell		
Heavy unlined jacket/shirt		
Footwear:		
Trail shoes		
Socks: wool or		
polypropylene		
Rain gear		

Other items I have found I need:

NOTES

REMINDERS

Trip date	Item	Done

Return: _____

Return: _____

Return: _____

Return: _____

Return: _____

Return: _____

Return: _____

Return: _____

Return: _____

Return: _____

Return: _____

Return: _____

Return: _____

Return: _____

Return: _____

Return: _____

REMINDERS

Trip date	Item	Done

Clean: _____

Clean: _____

Clean: _____

Clean: _____

Clean: _____

Clean: _____

Clean: _____

Clean: _____

Clean: _____

Clean: _____

Clean: _____

Clean: _____

Clean: _____

Clean: _____

Clean: _____

REMINDERS

Trip date	Item	Done

Repair:_____

Repair:_____

Repair:_____

Repair:_____

Repair:_____

Repair:_____

Repair:_____

Repair:_____

Repair:_____

Repair:_____

Repair:_____

Repair:_____

Repair:_____

Repair:_____

Repair:_____

Repair:_____

REMINDERS

	Trip date	Item	Done
Replace:			
Replace:			
Replace:			
Replace:			
Replace:			
Replace:			
Replace:			
Replace:			
Acquire:			
Acquire:			
Acquire:			
Acquire:			
Acquire:			
Acquire:			
Acquire:			

ADDRESSES

Name _____

Address _____

City, State and ZIP _____

Phone number _____

Contact person _____

Name _____

Address _____

City, State and ZIP _____

Phone number _____

Contact person _____

Name _____

Address _____

City, State and ZIP _____

Phone number _____

Contact person _____

Name _____

Address _____

City, State and ZIP _____

Phone number _____

Contact person _____

ADDRESSES

Name _____

Address _____

City, State and ZIP _____

Phone number _____

Contact person _____

Name _____

Address _____

City, State and ZIP _____

Phone number _____

Contact person _____

Name _____

Address _____

City, State and ZIP _____

Phone number _____

Contact person _____

Name _____

Address _____

City, State and ZIP _____

Phone number _____

Contact person _____

ADDRESSES

Name _____

Address _____

City, State and ZIP _____

Phone number _____

Contact person _____

Name _____

Address _____

City, State and ZIP _____

Phone number _____

Contact person _____

Name _____

Address _____

City, State and ZIP _____

Phone number _____

Contact person _____

Name _____

Address _____

City, State and ZIP _____

Phone number _____

Contact person _____

ADDRESSES

Name _____

Address _____

City, State and ZIP _____

Phone number _____

Contact person _____

Name _____

Address _____

City, State and ZIP _____

Phone number _____

Contact person _____

Name _____

Address _____

City, State and ZIP _____

Phone number _____

Contact person _____

Name _____

Address _____

City, State and ZIP _____

Phone number _____

Contact person _____

NOTES

NOTES

ORDER FORM

Cat's-paw Press
9561 Woodridge Circle
Eden Prairie, Minnesota 55347

Please send me _____ copy (copies) of *The Paddler's Planner*. I am enclosing $12.95 (plus $.78 sales tax, if in Minnesota) and $1.50 for shipping for each copy.

Please send me _____ copy (copies) of *Roughing It Elegantly: A Practical Guide To Canoe Camping*, by Patricia J. Bell. I am enclosing $9.95 (plus $.60 sales tax, if in Minnesota) and $1.50 for shipping for each copy.

Name _____

Address _____

_____

_____

Also from Cat's-paw Press:

Roughing It Elegantly: A Practical Guide To Canoe Camping

Enjoy North America's finest canoe wilderness elegantly — simply, efficiently, and with style. Pleasant, encouraging, environmentally-conscious...a sensible, personal discussion of canoe camping. **Library Journal**

"An excellent resource and reference book." **Minneapolis Star and Tribune**

"Offers the perspective of the ordinary camper who is also a woman." Eden Prairie (Minnesota) **Sailor**

"Outstanding... a primary reference...to get some idea of 'how to do a canoe trip.'" **Sawbill Canoe Outfitters**, Tofte, Minnesota

"The sort of book a guy gets for his woman if he wants her to go canoeing with him...book is full of sound advice on coping with the disasters that can occur" St. Paul (Minnesota) **Pioneer Press**

"Even beginners will feel at ease by following her well-explained, clear directions." Woodstock **Vermont Standard**

"Offers a wealth of practical tips and information...a valuable handguide for both experienced and not-so-experienced campers." Duluth (Minnesota) **News-Tribune**

"An outstanding guide to canoe camping...stylishly written...should appeal to all outdoor types." St. Cloud (Minnesota) **Daily Times**

"I could have used all the wonderful advice of **Roughing It Elegantly** when I first took to the woods. Moreover, my husband could have used the book, too." **Minnesota Reviews**

Shows how anyone can safely and comfortably enjoy a wilderness experience. Greg Leis, Executive Director, **Wilderness Inquiry**

ORDER FORM

Cat's-paw Press
9561 Woodridge Circle
Eden Prairie, Minnesota 55347

Please send me _____ copy (copies) of *The Paddler's Planner*. I am enclosing $12.95 (plus $.78 sales tax, if in Minnesota) and $1.50 for shipping for each copy.

Please send me _____ copy (copies) of *Roughing It Elegantly: A Practical Guide To Canoe Camping*, by Patricia J. Bell. I am enclosing $9.95 (plus $.60 sales tax, if in Minnesota) and $1.50 for shipping for each copy.

Name _____

Address _____

_____

_____

Also from Cat's-paw Press:

Roughing It Elegantly: A Practical Guide To Canoe Camping

Enjoy North America's finest canoe wilderness elegantly — simply, efficiently, and with style. Pleasant, encouraging, environmentally-conscious...a sensible, personal discussion of canoe camping. **Library Journal**

"An excellent resource and reference book." **Minneapolis Star and Tribune**

"Offers the perspective of the ordinary camper who is also a woman." Eden Prairie (Minnesota) **Sailor**

"Outstanding... a primary reference...to get some idea of 'how to do a canoe trip.'" **Sawbill Canoe Outfitters**, Tofte, Minnesota

"The sort of book a guy gets for his woman if he wants her to go canoeing with him...book is full of sound advice on coping with the disasters that can occur" St. Paul (Minnesota) **Pioneer Press**

"Even beginners will feel at ease by following her well-explained, clear directions." Woodstock **Vermont Standard**

"Offers a wealth of practical tips and information...a valuable handguide for both experienced and not-so-experienced campers." Duluth (Minnesota) **News-Tribune**

"An outstanding guide to canoe camping...stylishly written...should appeal to all outdoor types." St. Cloud (Minnesota) **Daily Times**

"I could have used all the wonderful advice of **Roughing It Elegantly** when I first took to the woods. Moreover, my husband could have used the book, too." **Minnesota Reviews**

Shows how anyone can safely and comfortably enjoy a wilderness experience. Greg Leis, Executive Director, **Wilderness Inquiry**